A Fox In The Yard

PARTHIAN

Peter J. Jones was born in Llanelli in 1945 and has worked in the public sector and overseas in the mining and oil industry. Since 1984, he has lived in the Llansteffan area where in the last few years he has resumed painting again. His paintings have been shown in solo exhibitions at leading galleries in Wales and Ireland. His university studies include education and Anglo-Welsh literature.

A Fox In
The Yard

Peter J. Jones

PARTHIAN

Parthian, Cardigan SA43 1ED
www.parthianbooks.com
Published with the financial support of the Welsh Books Council.
First published in 2017
© Peter J Jones
Cover design by R Harries
Cover image: The Reaper by Peter J Jones
Typeset by Elaine Sharples
Printed and bound Pulsio EU Sarl

Contents

Many of these poems are responses to events, places and characters connected with Wales, and some in particular to the Llansteffan area where I have been living for over thirty years.

Peter J. Jones

A Fox In The Yard

Julia
Sara
Watcyn

I still wonder why birds flying together in vast numbers and at great speeds do not collide, and how do they know when to start or to turn or to stop. Tudor Bevan, an outstanding teacher of literature who lived in Llansteffan was equally as curious to come up with the answer.

Lord's Park farm is beautifully set on the Llansteffan peninsula. The sheepdog there is aware of your presence even though he is unable to see you as you walk behind the hedge onto the cliff path some distance away. I imagine him to be knowing and content.

Sheepdog At Lord's Park

He is black and white on a hill
That sea downs embrace,
And is at one with himself
And affinity to place.

He hears footsteps before they fall,
And a breath rise
Before it calls
His name.

The sea falls, the sea rises,
There are no surprises so here he stays,
On earth as it is in heaven
At Lord's Park,
Llansteffan.

I was in Swansea station, a terminus, reading a letter from a girlfriend telling me why our romance should end. It was a time when flowers blossomed on railway platforms.

All Change

Diesel engines warming
In this winter terminus
Anticipate the subtle curves
Of track and space
Between us.

I read your letter,
And those lilies on platform two
Momentarily
Were you in a white dress
With petals waving on your fingers
Adieu.

A fox entered my yard and in no hurry carried out a personal inspection of what was about. An old scythe attracted his interest and he returned to it a number of times, and finally as if giving it his approval, he faded into the shadows.

Fox In The Yard

Moon about
That fox at night
So dark and green and glistening,
See that fox head
Dip the light
To sniff the scythe blade and the run
Of every silhouette and sound
Soft pillowing down
The farm.

Dai Lodwick was a skilled mechanic, and a very likeable character who lived in Llansteffan. He used to repair my Morris Minor and often gave me the impression that when I left it in his yard he would soon be verbally challenging the car to start. It always did.

Top Mechanical

He was top mechanical,
Fluent in Morris and Jaguar
And spectacular
With oxyacetylene.

He was a metal expressionist
Dabbling in gunk and piston light,
And could frighten a boxful of dynamite
Down his pit full of confrontation.
"valves buggered, she's burning oil,
Cylinder's f…' and so is the coil".

He was top mechanical,
He cut his own umbilical
With welding gear.
His constant fear was swearing at God,
And the inevitability of rust.

Down the street where I was born was Llanelli steelworks with its shunting engines, sparks, furnaces and the warm waters of the steelworks pond full of goldfish. Beyond the pond was Stradey woods, as children we knew every tree and trail and seemed to play our lives away there throughout the summer.

Being Young And Full Of Summer

Being young and full of summer
Was to wake on the run
To the steelworks pond.
The waters were warm,
And fishes of gold tailed
Our shadows on the reeds
And the wagons sparking to the docks
And the dock- filled tides beyond.

Being young and full of summer
Was to chase our breath
Down the dog- boned lanes
To the woods deepening in ash and elm,
And there our secrets tell
To the listening pools and the river gurgling our names
Down the brown- legged runs
To the sea.

As a child I remember an old character who would suddenly appear and stay in the area for a few weeks. Local people acknowledged him, he was a part of the place. His clothes were torn, his hair long and his coat tied by cord. I thought he was some kind of magician.

Hand Of The Wild Hawthorn

The stranger's coat was scarecrow spun
Round thorn and rips of fur,
And the cats ran out and the dogs played dumb
As he whispered at the bar,
I can hold a rising moon
Upon a rabbit's paw,
And tell you secrets of the shells
That roll on the sea-tongued shore.
God bless, he sighed,
As he dipped his glass
Like the wind dips a curl of corn,
And the hand he placed upon the door
Was the hand of the wild hawthorn.

Swallows arrive to tell of spring, and they stay for the summer and the harvest, and then leave for Africa before the winter settles in. Perhaps when horses worked the land there was a closer and more natural connection to the seasons than today.

Seasons

The touch of spring on sleeping earth
Awakes the forces in the dell,
And strong is the hand the horses feel
To the pull of a seed hung bell.

Harvest rising on a swallow tail
Divining to the sun,
And fields of gold are bellying
As autumn shadows run.

Breath of winter glistening
On the skin of mountain bone,
And the oak child in the acorn
Feels the horses moving home.

This happened many years ago. I remember a friend telling me that in time I would have a better understanding, a greater empathy with others on matters of grief and loss.

New White Shirt

It is the morning of your funeral, Mam,
And damn my new white shirt's to iron
And bread to cut so clean and thin
To resonate the ring of china.
The phone goes, someone selling double glazing,
And my sister, softly reads the labels on the flowers,
And Dad staring at the hours of the clock
And polishing his shoes again,
Evading.

Later, men crowded out the kitchen
For beer, fags and anecdotes of Mam,
And I laughed with them but felt alone
Like that last train home from Paddington.
Then voices slowly faded as women peered in to say
C'mon love we'd better go
We'll miss the traffic on the motorway.

Sitting on the step that night and Dai passes,
A colossal man who took the whisky hard
Since the passing of his son. He shook my hand
And looked down from the stars to say:
You'll be stronger now this day is out
'Cause you will understand see boy
Just what that white shirt's all about.

As a child in primary school I remember illustrating these dates on a calendar and using the words, star, cross, silver and Bethlehem.

Notes In A Calendar

Good Friday   make a cross
                           from oak and elm,
                           cut in the words
                           faith be,
                           amen.

Easter Sunday   clean the wounds
                           bless this time,
                           break the bread
                           share the wine.

Christmas Eve   make a star
                           a silvered gem
                           silhouetting
                           Bethlehem.

The person referred to is the distinguished writer and poet Glyn Jones who loved the Llansteffan area, and whose work was influenced by his lasting relationship with the place. I knew Glyn Jones through an introduction by his friends Diana and Tudor Bevan of Llansteffan.

Haven

And he did seek
A place to love
To hone his gift within,
And through his words he held our time
In easy, sweet imagining.

That place
Is on a western down
Where Towy meets the sea,
And he did find his spirit there
To grace the estuary.

Beyond Llyn Brianne dam and beside the river Camddwr on the mountain road to Tregaron is the chapel Soar Y Mynydd. The chapel remains open, and the gravestone of Evan and Anne is near the entrance.

Non Conformity

High on the wind
A hawk pinned by God
Unravels mice from fern and sheep
And the shadows of the farms
Drowned deep in the stillness of a dam.

Beyond the dam clear waters of a river
Run to the bow of birch and pine,
And there at the ford a long white chapel
Still divines a beam
For non conformity.

Anne and Evan at rest here,
Beneath a stone
That dips from mountain rain,
But hush, hush now
As they waken to their wedding day again.

Evan listening to the round of wheels
And the ponies snorting at the ford,
Anne startling in her white dress
And her vows
In whisper to the lord.
Evan so warm and Gallilean
Keeping out the cold,
Turning down the lamp of oil
As her wedding dress unfolds.

Hush, they are sleeping now
As the stars light the face of this land,
Hush, for so rare is the peace here,
Understand.

Kusha Petts was a gifted painter who lived in Llansteffan. We met when I first arrived there in 1984. A few years later we opened a gallery on the village square. I remember with affection the cups of tea, the driftwood fire and the ever present paints and oils.

Tea With Kusha

Come in,
Her smile eclipses mine.
Come in, I'm painting seas
Seas of blue
This time.

We sit
Around the driftwood hiss and hum,
We talk Matisse
Share the welshcakes
Pick the crumbs.

Come see me soon
I touch cerulean fingers,
The waft of linseed on her skin
Still lingers.

Driving home one night I felt a nudge, the slightest of touches on the steering wheel. Passing by the same place the following day there was a badger dead on the wayside. Sometimes when I drive this road I feel that touch again.

Badger Down

Never saw his black and silver
Shuffling down the night,
Never felt his life exploding
Heart beat racing
Dynamite.

Next morning breaking
Saw his curled form
Crimson smudging on his head,
Now I feel him
On the wheel spin
Wildness living
Wildness dead

The friend is Colwyn Morris, a renowned stained glass designer from Llanelli. He lived alone and spent much of his life after the second world war working from his London studio. Tough, independent and intellectual are appropriate words to describe him. He died in hospital at Carmarthen. At his funeral I remember on the coffin his army uniform with the distinctive Desert Rat motif on the shoulder patches.

Hospital Admission

Molecule of friend,
His hair stuck out
At the back of his head
Like the nape of a finch
On a wreath
In bed.

How casually he ticked
The boxes for admission,
Occupation....... desert rat: El Alamein,
                        artist: stained glass design.
Allergies.............tinned fruit and vegan quiche,
                        second homes, the nouveau-riche,
                        public schools and mobile phones,
                        and fear of not being left alone.

So quietly he laid
With indifference and with love,
As death upon the sinew snaps
The hawk within the dove

Asleep
He dreams of fluttering wings
Through sparkling glass
As a bird to his god
Returning.

Seeing one taking a fish is unbelievable,
until you see it again.

Sea Hawk

Cross bow imagery of flight,
Sea-flung arrow
Sea-flung light,
Spin of wing
Suck of claw,
Air to water
Meteor.

I recall the walk I took from Llanybri to Llangynog war memorial on a Remembrance Sunday. I wondered whether some of those who fell in the 1st World War, and who are named on the memorial stone, would have walked the same path and perhaps played as boys in the woods passed Coomb. The reference to Mametz Wood relates to the strong Welsh involvement in the fierce battle fought there in 1916 at heavy cost.

Took I Your Breath

Took I your breath
When yours had gone,
And now I take the winding road
Where once as young you called and played
Along the wooded stream passed Coomb.
But I was dumb to tell you of the darkening calls
From Mametz Wood and Passchendaele
To come.

Took I my stance
When you did fall,
And now before this poppied stone
I hear sweet music call your names
Beyond the listening trees of Coomb.
And I am free to walk with you
Along the peace trails that you laid
For my return.

As silence falls upon this place
Take you my thanks
Take I your grace.

Christmas Eve, several years ago I was at home in my studio in Llansteffan painting. The stranger at my door was to become my wife.

Llansteffan – December 24th

Alone,
A painter
Cuts the canvas grain,
And touches on a star new born
Through dark and wild clouds
Breaking.

There at his door a stranger stands
So devastating in her coat
Of silver down,
And she foretells of what is gathered
Or what is lost in love
Can still be found.

Then she did hold that new born star
Until all gathering was done,
And there in silvering coat
With him she stayed
For love,
For love's continuum.

Seven Days

Buying faggots in Llansteffan,
Tudor Bevan asked me why the rooks there
Fly on such tight coordinates.
I promised him the answer
In seven days.

On day four I wrote:
dusk on the day's bell rings in the head of rooks,
they hear as one, and drawn from hilt of copse
they run the wind's song down to oak
and then to elm returning.

Day five, picking cockles on the Point,
I considered seas and the rock and pull of planets
And I saw centuries of rooks, a black shawl spun
Round the turning of the moon and the turning of the sun,
Then I added: rooks as black swords spinning in the sky
yet never touching
touching never,
as if to touch to die.

In my garden on the sixth
The radio flickered as the rooks swept by,
And later, digging earth
With my head bowed to the spade and the sheen of worms,
They soared again in counterpoint to the sound of Bach
And my scattering of seeds.
Moments later I was writing:
see their shadows on the marigolds, black and orange fading as
the dahlias take their rise,
and deep within the jasmine see the imageries of spring
rook shadows crossed on snowdrops bring.

On the seventh in the bar of the Sticks
Tudor fixed upon the making of a black shawl spun
To the weave of wings and my scattering of seeds.
Interesting, interesting indeed he sighed,
And when asked about the rock and pull of planets
I could hear that clock start ticking in his head,
Give me seven days, yes seven days, he said.